1

1   Introduction

A number of recent studies have found a repeating asymmetric, cyclical pattern in retail gasoline prices which can be described as a sharp and relatively large price increase followed by smaller and more gradual price decreases. This type of pricing pattern corresponds with that predicted by Maskin and Tirole (1988) in their theoretical Edgeworth price cycle model. Their model examines a sequential pricing game between two firms selling a homogenous good. A large price increase, or "restoration," by one firm is followed by the other firm with subsequent decreases, or "cheating," until the price is close to marginal cost which triggers another restoration. This model implicitly suggests some form of price leadership.

In this paper, we examine how widespread and persistent price cycling is in the United States over a twelve year period (from 1996-2007) for 350 cities covering all 50 states and the District of Columbia using daily retail price data. While other studies such as Doyle *et al.* (2010) and Lewis (2009) examine data on gasoline pricing in the U.S. and find price cycling a Midwestern phenomenon, a finding we confirm, our data set is long enough that the earlier observations predate cycling. Specifically, our results show that the recent price cycles began in 2000 and generally occur in seven states located in PADD 2 (Midwest): Illinois, Indiana, Kentucky, Michigan, Minnesota, Missouri, and Ohio. Prior to 2000, we find no cities with cycling behavior. This is the first paper that has been able to identify when cycling in the Midwest began and which cities began to cycle first.

Consequently, we can examine prices in cycling cities relative to non-cycling cities before and after the appearance of cycling in our data. Other researchers have been able to examine whether cycling is ultimately harmful or beneficial to consumers using a cross sectional analysis, *e.g.*, Doyle *et al.* (2010); we are able to analyze this question using panel data and a difference in differences framework. We find consumers are better off on average in cities after they began cycling by one cent per gallon. This finding is consistent with the hypothesis that price cycling is a form of retail price war, as was the case with prior documented episodes of price cycling in the U.S. during the 1970's.[1]

Additionally, we address the question of what factors explain why city-level retail gasoline prices cycle. While we do not have a time series of market structure variables, we examine a cross-section of a sample of cycling and non-cycling cities for the period when cycling began. Prior work has examined factors such as the concentration of independents (Lewis, 2009) and possible price leadership by large retail chains (Speedway and QuikTrip) in the Midwest (Lewis, 2011). Other studies highlight the role of large, branded retailers (*e.g.*, Noel 2007a) or the concentration of major brands and independents with convenience stores (Doyle *et al.*, 2010).

Previous research, however, has not separately examined the role of ownership structure amongst branded retailers. Within this group, ownership structures can vary from complete vertical integration (in the case of a refiner's company-owned-and-operated stations) to third-party control (*e.g.*, so-called "open dealer" or "jobber" stations). If, as previous research suggests, it is the centralization (or "coordination") of pricing decisions of branded retailers that facilitates cycling, then refiner company-ops should be correlated with the presence of cycling given that upstream refiners have *direct* control over the pricing patterns at these stations. Using data on ownership concentration, our results confirm this hypothesis; specifically, we find that the ownership concentration of direct refiner-operated stations (but not their raw market share) is correlated with more cycling. On the other hand, the raw share of "independent" retailers (but not their concentration) positively correlates with the presence of cycling. These results also appear consistent with the underlying theory of Edgeworth cycles.

The next section of the paper reviews the literature. The third section details the data and the methodology used to identify price cycles. The fourth section examines the price effects of cycling using a difference in differences estimator. The fifth section examines possible causes of cycling. The sixth section of the paper presents conclusions.

---

[1] See Allvine & Patterson (1974) and Castanias & Johnson (1993).

2   Literature review

Most prior studies examining Edgeworth cycles in retail gasoline prices have looked at Australian, Canadian, or U.S. data. In some of the Australian and Canadian cases, researchers have found that cycling is associated with either suggested or confirmed tacit collusion (Wang, 2009) or explicit collusion (Wang, 2008; Erutku & Hildebrand, 2010).

In other cases, researchers have not linked price cycling patterns explicitly to collusion. Eckert (2003) and Noel (2007b) find that cycling behavior is more prevalent in Canadian cities that have relatively more small firms. Noel (2007a) and Eckert & West (2004) find that in Canada price increases tend to be led by the larger firms and price decreases tend to be led by smaller firms. Eckert (2002) finds that price cycles in Windsor, Ontario, may result in the observation of asymmetric pass through. Atkinson (2009) examines prices in Guelph, Ontario, and finds very distinct, recurring price cycles.

In terms of evidence of price cycling in U.S. cities, Allvine & Patterson (1974) describe a "yo-yo pattern" (p. 243) in prices for a number of mostly western U.S. cities at various intervals between 1971-1973. The cycles in each city end sometime in 1972 or 1973, which coincided with the lead up to the 1973 oil shortage. Castanias & Johnson (1993) present some summary statistics on price cycles in Los Angeles in 1968-1972 which show a similar pattern.

Lewis (2009) examines the price reaction of cycling and non-cycling cities to the 2005 hurricanes. Using 18 months of data from 2004-2005 covering 85 cities in the Eastern half of the U.S., he finds that price cycling cities are concentrated in the Midwestern U.S. and tend to be associated with higher concentrations of independent gas stations. He also finds that cost changes are passed through more quickly in cities where retail gasoline prices follow an Edgeworth price cycle pattern. Lewis and Noel (2011) further examine asymmetric pass through in 90 cities, some cycling and some not, and find that cycling cities have quicker pass through of cost changes from wholesale to retail than non-cycling cities, which is a similar conclusion to Lewis (2009).

Doyle *et al.* (2010) examine 115 U.S. cities for cycling for a one year period from 2000-2001 and find that cycling tends to be concentrated in the Midwest. The authors focus on concentration of independent gas stations with convenience stores and the presence of brands as potential explanations for the prevalence of price cycling. Their main finding is that the most concentrated and the least concentrated markets are less likely to cycle. They also find some evidence that cities with at least two major brands present are more likely to cycle. Finally, Doyle *et al.* find price cycling cities are weakly associated with lower retail prices.

Finally, Lewis (2011) examines 280 U.S. cities for cycling with data from 2004-2010. He suggests that price leadership by independent gas stations with centralized city-wide pricing, Speedway and QuikTrip, generates the cycling pattern in many Midwestern cities. He also examines Speedway data to show that in a number of cities Speedway tends to lead the price increases.

3   Retail gasoline price cycles in U.S. cities

We use daily average regular grade retail gasoline price data for 350 cities covering all 50 states and the District of Columbia from February 1996 to December 2007. These price data come from the Oil Price Information Service (OPIS) and are generated from a sample of retail outlets that accept fleet/credit cards. In general more than 50 percent of stations in any city are observed on any given day. We subtract the gasoline taxes from the retail price data.

Recent studies documenting price cycling over a significant number of cities generally use one of two methods to identify cycling cities. One approach is to use a Markov switching regression model based on transition probabilities; *e.g.*, Noel (2007b) utilizes this identification method. Alternatively, Lewis (2009, 2011) and Doyle *et al.* (2010) use the median value of retail price changes to detect price cycles.[2] The idea being that price cycle cities will have relatively more negative price change observations than positive ones; thus, the median value of cycling

---

[2] Similarly, Eckert (2003) counts the number of first differences in retail prices that are equal to zero, where cities with a relatively low count of zeros are considered price cycle cities.

cities will be negative. Additionally, the median change will be larger (in absolute value) when the typical daily price decline is larger.

Table 1 details the geographic coverage of our price data as well as providing summary statics on prices. The states are grouped by PADD (Petroleum Administration for Defense Districts) and subdivisions for PADD 1 (East Coast). The number of cities in each state is listed as well as the mean price and median price change for three periods: (1) the full sample period, 1996-2007; (2) the period before price cycling began, 1996-1999;[3] and (3) the period after price cycling began, 2001-2007. The median first difference for the pre-cycle period, 1996-1999, is mostly zero or close to zero for most states outside of PADD 2 with the exception of a few states in PADD 5. Even for PADD 2 and PADD 5, the median first difference is generally only a few hundredths of a cent less than zero. When examining the median difference for the post-cycle period, 2001-2007, most states outside PADD 2 still have median differences close to zero (although, few are actually equal to zero) while the median difference for many states in PADD 2 are well below zero including Illinois, Indiana, Kentucky, Michigan, Minnesota, and Ohio.

In Table 2, we list each of the 52 cities (grouped into 9 states) in our sample that cycled for at least one year. We use Doyle *et al.*'s (2010) median first difference cutoff value of -0.5 cents or lower to identify the existence of price cycling. We grouped years 1996-1999 together since no cycling occurred during this period. In 2000, 5 cities in Ohio had prices that cycled: Akron, Canton, Columbus, Dayton, and Toledo. Just one year later in 2001, 40 cities across 8 states had prices that cycled.

Broadly, in order to categorize a city as a "cycling" city for purposes of our difference in differences estimation in Section 4, we took the median value of the first difference over the entire post-cycle period, 2001-07, to classify a city as cycling or not.[4] This approach excludes

---

[3] See the discussion of Table 2 below for details on the identification of the start of price cycling.
[4] While we have the same retail price data for 2008-2010, this later period has sustained periods of general price declines caused primarily by the collapse in crude oil prices. Using either method for identifying cycles during a period of general price declines leads to false positives for price cycling.

cities that cycled for only a year or two. The result is that 34 of 350 cities cycled during this period. In addition to using a median price difference measure of identification, we also use a Markov switching regression model to identify cycling cities. The Markov model estimates two transition probabilities based on Neftçi (1984): (a) the probability of three continuous days of price increases and (b) the probability of three continuous days of price decreases. If (a) < (b) with statistical significance, then the city is considered a cycling city.[5] The last column of Table 2 provides the results of the Markov test. The median and Markov tests identify similar sets of cities; although, the Markov test is more inclusive and identifies 46 cycling cities at the 5% level and 51 cities at the 10% level.[6]

In sum, Table 2 indicates that the recent episodes of cycling in the U.S. began sometime in 2000 and is primarily a Midwestern phenomenon. In an effort to better understand the 2000 transition from non-cycling to cycling, in Figure 1 we plot the price paths of the five cities in Ohio that began cycling in 2000 as they move from a non-cycling to a cycling equilibrium . In the two years before 2000, while there were noticeable spikes in the first difference on two separate occasions, the median first difference generally fluctuated between 0 and -0.5 cents. However, after a dramatic drop in the median values for the 5 cities in mid-2000, the new median path generally had values fluctuating between -0.5 and -1.5, which is a much more wider band than before mid-2000.

---

[5] See the Appendix for further details on the Markov switching model.

[6] There are nine cities that the Markov model identifies at cycling that are not listed in Table 2. At the five percent level, the additional cities are St. Louis, IL; Detroit, MI; and Charleston, WV. At the ten percent level, the additional cities also include Kankakee, IL; Des Moines, IA; Santa Fe, NM; Brownsville, TX; Corpus Christie, TX; and Parkersburg, WV.

4 Average retail gasoline price differences across cycling and non-cycling cities

Some of the research examining price cycling, primarily in Australia and Canada, have described or suggested either explicit or tacit collusion (*e.g.*, Wang, 2008, Erutku and Hildebrand, 2010) while other papers have suggested or shown that Edgeworth cycles are price/welfare improving relative to more constant cost pass through regimes (*e.g.*, Noel, 2009a; Doyle *et al.*, 2010; Lewis and Noel, 2011). In this section, we examine whether retail prices are on average higher or lower in cycling than non-cycling cities by utilizing before and after data from cycling and non-cycling cities.

For the difference in differences estimator, we use the Markov list of price cycling cities from Table 2, at both the 5% ("the shorter list") and 10% levels ("the longer list").[7] The short list identifies price cycling cities only in the Midwest whereas the longer list identifies more cycling cities in the Midwest and adds a few cities from the Gulf Coast states.

Using the daily price data from 1996-2007 and 1996-2010, we examine the average price difference between cities that began price cycling in 2000 verses those that did not, before and after the advent of price cycling.[8] We do this comparison with city and year fixed effects, with the smaller and larger list of cycling cities and then restrict the cities examined (both cycling and non-cycling) to just the Midwest and Gulf Coast. Table 3 presents the results of estimating these variations on the following regression:

$$p_{i,t} = \alpha + \beta_1 \, CycleAfter_{i,t} + \beta_2 \, Cycle_i + \beta_3 \, After_t + \sum_{y=4}^{n} \beta_y D_{yt} + \sum_{s=n+1}^{n+51} \beta_s D_{st} + \varepsilon_{i,t} \quad (1)$$

where $p_{i,t}$ denotes the average price in the *i*-th city for *t*-th day. The dummy variable $Cycle_i$ takes a value of one if the city cycles after 2000. The dummy variable $After_t$ takes a value of one

---

[7] The median first difference test identifies a similar set of cities as the Markov 5% test and the difference in differences results are similar using the median approach.

[8] In this analysis we use data from 1996-2010. Due to the sizeable and long lasting price decreases in 2008 we only used the 1996-2007 data to identify cycling cities.

if the year is after 2000. The dummy variable $CycleAfter_{it}$ is the interaction of those two dummy variables and takes on a value of one if the city is a cycling city and it is after 2000.[9] Thus, a negative estimate of the coefficient β_3 implies that the regime change from not cycling to cycling is correlated with a decrease in the average price in cycling cities relative to the non-cycling cities. The variables α_i, and $\varepsilon_{i,t}$ represent the constant term and the error term, respectively. For all the specifications we used standard errors clustered by state. The other dummy variables represent the year and state fixed effects. The number of years used changes the number of year fixed effects.

Columns (1) and (2) of Table 3 show the estimated effect of cycling using the shorter list of cycling cities for 1996-2010 and 1996-2007, respectively. The results show that prices decreased in cycling cities relative to non-cycling cities by approximately 1 cent per gallon. The effect using the shorter data set lacks statistically significant at conventional levels. Columns (3) and (4) use the longer list of cycle cites and show very similar results to that of the shorter list of cycle cities.

The results presented in columns (5), (6), (7), and (8) are calculated using a smaller control group. No longer are the prices in cycling cities, which in the case of the short list are all in the Midwest and the longer list including some Gulf Coast cities, compared with cities through out the entire country. In these regressions the control cities are located in the same PADD as the cycle cities. The results in column (5) and (6) compare the relative price change in the cycling cities identified using the five percent Markov criteria with the other cities in PADD 2 with the two different time periods. The results show a somewhat larger statistically significant decrease in prices, 1.4 and 1.3 cents per gallon, in cycling cities once they began cycling but it is generally the same order of magnitude as the previous results. The results in column (7) and (8) were

---

[9] We used the year 2001 for the beginning of cycling since it looks like cycling began in mid 2000 for most cities and all of the cycling cities were cycling by 2001. The analysis was not sensitive to the exact date. As a robustness check we used 2000 as the beginning of cycling and found very similar results.

generated by comparing the longer list of cycling cities to all the cities in PADDs 2 and 3. While the relative price decline is smaller, the effect of the change remains between ¾ of a cent and 1 cent per gallon.

The parameter estimates using the larger and the smaller data set are very similar but the effects are somewhat smaller using the shorter time period and are generally not statistically significant. This difference may be due to two factors. One, there are a little over 20 percent less observations in the smaller data set. Two, the later three years of data include the collapse of the price of crude oil in 2008. Lewis and Noel (2011), Noel (2009a), and Lewis (2009) point out that cycle cities have quicker pass thru of cost shocks than the non-cycle cities. The results using the longer data set would include this quicker pass through of the negative cost shock which would have shown up in the cycling cities.

These results strongly suggest that the advent of price cycling lead to a 1 cent per gallon reduction in relative prices in cycling cities. While other research, *e.g.*, Doyle *et al.* (2010), has suggested based on cross sectional variation that cycling leads to lower prices, we were able to analyze prices before and after cycling in cycling cities. In addition, as others such as Noel (2009b) have mentioned, these are average effects assuming that consumers make uniform purchases over time and do not take advantage of the price cycles. If consumers can take advantage of the cycles, price savings may be greater.

5   Explaining the presence of retail gasoline price cycles: station ownership characteristics

Several recent studies have examined the role that station characteristics (*e.g.*, Doyle *et al.*, 2010) or general ownership structure (*e.g.*, Noel, 2007b; Lewis, 2009) play in explaining the presence of retail gasoline price cycling. The latter studies stress the influence that "independents," *i.e.*, gasoline stations (or networks thereof) that are not affiliated with a petroleum refiner. In general, these studies find that a larger number or proportion of independent stations in a local market correlates with the presence of price cycling and that these players tend

10

to be the firms that initiate and "lead down" the market during the undercutting phase of the cycle.

While the presence or concentration of independent gasoline stations may be an important determinant of gasoline price cycling, it is possible that the concentration of vertically integrated stations also plays a significant role. For example, while independent stations tend to drive undercutting, integrated stations might largely explain the other side of the coin: namely, initiation of the relenting phase. The ability to lead market prices upwards after hitting the bottom of a cycle may be a function of being able to set prices simultaneously at a large number of stations (*e.g.*, Noel 2007a), a characteristic that applies especially to fully integrated branded stations.[10] We expand on this theme by examining the influence of large, refiner company-owned-and-company-operated (COCO) networks of retail stations on a city's propensity to cycle. These are the stations at which upstream refiners are able to exert the most direct control over downstream retail prices. Accounting for the presence of both refiner-COCO stations and independent stations networks allows us to examine the separate relative contributions that each makes in determining the presence of city-level retail gasoline price cycling.

In order to examine causes of price cycling, we use data on station ownership characteristics. These data, which are obtained from New Image Marketing, Ltd. for 31 cities (18 cycling plus 13 non-cycling) provide information on brand market shares and ownership structure within the brands.[11] These data reflect a census of gasoline stations in the selected cities.[12] Three

---

[10] Gas stations that sell branded gas may be owned and operated by individuals who basically operate franchises (lessee-dealer stations); may be owned by the major oil company (refiner-COCO stations); or may be owned by the major oil company and leased to an operator that sets the retail price (open-dealers). Refiners only indirectly set the retail prices posted at their lessee-dealers stations (through the DTW) and open-dealer/jobber stations (through the branded rack price). As discussed below, the extent to which refiners can influence retail prices is almost certainly greater at the former.

[11] The 31 select cities (grouped by state) are as follows—AZ: Phoenix; CA: Los Angeles, San Francisco; CO: Denver; FL: Miami; GA: Atlanta; IL: Chicago, Peoria, Rockford, Springfield; IN: Terre Haute; KY: Lexington, Louisville; LA: New Orleans; MA: Boston; MI: Detroit, Grand Rapids, Kalamazoo; MN: Minneapolis; MO: St. Louis; NJ: Newark; OH: Cleveland, Toledo; TN: Knoxville, Memphis, Nashville; TX: Dallas, Houston; UT: Salt Lake City; VA: Fairfax; WA: Seattle.

[12] It was not possible to obtain the New Image data across all 350 cities used in the previous analyses as the company does not survey most cities. The 31 select cities correspond to all of the available surveys

ownership structures/groups, indexed by O, are reflected in the New Image data: (1) refiner-COCOs; (2) the sum of independent and branded jobber sites;[13] and (3) lessee-dealer sites. Because data on lessee dealer sites is not available for each of the 31 cities, we consider only refiner-COCO and independent stations in the following analysis.[14]

Let $s_{i,O}^{(f)} \in (0,1]$ denote the share of total retail gasoline sales made in city i through stations of "flag" (or brand) $f = 1, ..., F$ that are operated under ownership structure O.[15] Define

$$HHI_{i,O} = \sum_{f=1}^{F} (s_{i,O}^{(f)})^2 \in (0,1] \qquad (2)$$

as the Herfindahl-Hirschman Index (HHI) of "within-group" (*i.e.*, stations of type O) retail gasoline sales in city i. $s_{i,O}^{(f)}$ is the share of city-wide gasoline sales sold through stations operating under a given flag-ownership configuration.[16] The possible values of $HHI_{i,O}$ range from a maximum of 1.0 to a minimum based on the specific distribution of the relevant flag shares. The $HHI_{i,O}$ approaches one as the as the number of flags decreases or the disparity in the size between flags (holding the number of flags constant) increases.

Using the above HHIs we estimate the following cross-sectional probit regression:

$$\Pr(Cycle_i = 1) = \Phi(\alpha + \sum_O (\beta_{HHI} HHI_{i,O} + \beta_s s_{i,O}) + \Gamma X_i), \qquad (3)$$

---

conducted by New Image that could be reasonably matched to our pricing data. For most select cities the census is from 2000 or 2001 with the remainder in 1999. Since our previous results suggest the cities were consistently cycling, and because brand and ownership shares tend to be stable, we do not see this limitation as problematic.

[13] Separate data for independent and branded jobber sites are not available.

[14] Because refiners can effectively "determine" the margin earned by their lessee-dealers (through perturbations of the DTW price assessed to a specific dealer), the pricing outcomes at these stations will tend to much closer to refiner-COCOs than to open-dealer/jobber stations (who acquire wholesale supply at posted branded rack prices). As such, we do not view the exclusion of lessee-dealer stations from the analysis or the grouping of jobbers along with independents to be problematic.

[15] For example, in a given city i we might observe the following flag-ownership configurations:
$$\{f = Shell; O = refiner\text{-}COCO\} \text{ (group 1)};$$
$$\{f = Shell; O = jobber\} \text{ (group 2)};$$
$$\{f = QuickTrip; O = independent\} \text{ (group 3)}.$$

[16] City- and flag/ownership-level retail gasoline sales volume estimates are also obtained from New Image.

where $Cycle_i$ is an indicator taking a value of one if (based on the 10 percent Markov rule) city i is designated as a price cycling city and zero otherwise.[17] The variable Φ denotes the standard normal distribution function, while α denotes the intercept term. By assumption, the regression error term under the above framework is $\varepsilon_{i,O} \sim N(0,1)$.

The variable X_i denotes a vector of city-level Census demographic controls (median household income, population density, total population), and Γ denotes a vector of coefficients. β_{HHI} and β_s are the primary coefficients of interest. If, e.g., $\beta_{HHI} > 0$, then a higher concentration of within-group sales pertaining to ownership structure O is positively correlated with the probability that retail gasoline price cycling occurs in city i, all else equal (and *vice versa*).

Table 4 presents the results of estimating variations of equation (3). Columns (1) and (2) control only for the HHI and market share measures, respectively. Since the marginal effect of concentration may vary by different compositions of refiner and independent networks across cities, column (3) combines the HHI and share measure into a single specification. Finally, column (4) adds the additional controls in X_i to the specifications in column (3).

All of the reported probit coefficient estimates in Table 4 are presented in terms of their marginal effects. Robust (heteroskedasticity-consistent) z-statistics are shown in parentheses. The coefficient estimate on the HHI of within-group sales of refiner COCO stations in column (1) is statistically significant and indicates that a 100-point increase in the HHI is associated with a 1.3 percentage point increase in the probability that a city exhibits cycling behavior.[18] The HHI for independent retailers is positively correlated with cycling but not statistically significant.

---

[17] As a robustness check, equation (3) was also estimated with a 5 percent cut-off for the Markov model. This stricter threshold resulted in only one less sample city (Chicago) being classified as cycling and had very little effect on the estimations.

[18] The HHIs used in estimating the regressions presented in Table 4 are defined continuously on the unit interval (*i.e.*, the HHIs are scaled by 10,000).

Column (2) shows that the refiner market share coefficient is positive but not significantly related to cycling. However, the independents' market share is positive and statistically significant. A one percentage point increase in this share is associated with a 1.3 percentage point increase in the probability of cycling. Note also that the magnitude of the point estimate on the independent share is appreciably larger than that pertaining to refiner share.

Controlling for both the HHI and market share measure concurrently has little effect on the results. Again, only the HHI (market share) of the refiner-affiliated (independent) firms is statistically significant, and the magnitude of the marginal effect is comparable to column (1). Similarly, controlling for other city-specific factors (column (4)) has little qualitative effect on the results, although the various HHI and market share effects are somewhat larger in magnitude. In this specification a 100 point increase in the refiner HHI is associated with a 1.5 percentage point increase in the probability of cycling, while a 1.0 percentage point increase in the market share of independent stations implies a 2.1 percentage point increase in the probability of cycling.

What should one take from the results in Table 4? While we cannot relate our city-level market structure variables directly to any meaningful price measure across cities, the results in Table 4 can be viewed as broadly consistent with the previous theoretical (Eckert, 2003; Noel, 2008) and empirical literatures (Noel, 2007a, 2007b; Lewis, 2009). Our finding that within-refiner concentration, but not overall market share, positively correlates with cycling appears generally consistent with the underlying theory of Edgeworth cycles formulated by Maskin & Tirole (1988). Since cycles in this (and previous) studies appear to reflect city-wide pricing movements, those price changes must be effectively 'coordinated' at the city level. Indeed, a central behavioral prediction associated with the presence of Edgeworth cycles in retail gasoline is that "larger firms have a greater incentive and greater coordinating ability to trigger a new round of relenting phases . . . ." (Noel, 2007a, p. 84). To the extent that this same "coordinating ability" is increasing in the within-group HHI of integrated stations, our results are consistent with this notion. On the other hand, since a high *overall* market share of integrated stations does

14

not necessarily imply that any given station is appreciably larger (or more significant) than any other, it may not be surprising that the raw share of integrated stations does not correlate with cycling.

Our finding that a greater presence of independent retailers—as measured by their overall market share—generally increases the propensity for cycling, but not so concentration, also aligns with prior research. These results are qualitatively similar to Lewis (2011) despite the somewhat differing classification of "independent" stations.[19] When controlling for state fixed effects and/or flag-specific shares, Lewis finds a marginally significant positive effect of the independents' HHI on cycling or a statistically insignificant negative effect. The overall share of independents, however, is positive and statistically significant in his most fully specified model.

6   Concluding remarks

Our analysis of U.S. retail price data confirms the finding in the literature that retail price cycling is generally a phenomenon of the upper Midwest. Our analysis is the first however, to detail when cycling started, mid-2000, and that it continues unabated.[20] Depending on the method/criteria for identifying price cycles, there are some cities outside the Midwest that have retail price cycles. In addition we show that the two main methods used in the literature to identify price cycles give very similar result.

With respect to the consequences of gasoline price cycles, we find that the average price in cycling cites declined relative to non-cycling cities once cycling commenced. Using multiple criteria for indentifying cities with price cycles and multiple control groups we show approximately a 1 cent per gallon decline in the average price in cycling cities relative to non-cycling cities once cycling begins. As Noel (2009b) points out, the average price difference for

---

[19] For instance, Lewis classifies Speedway as an independent dealer, whereas we classify it as refiner-COCO outlet since it is directly owned and controlled by a petroleum refiner (Marathon/Ashland).
[20] We have continued to analyze the retail prices and through the end of 2010 the Midwestern cities that we identify as cycling still have retail price cycles.

cycling cites may underestimate the consumer effects of price cycling since consumers may be able to take advantage of the cycling and make counter cyclical purchases.

With respect to the causes of retail price cycling, we find evidence that the concentration of branded refiner company-owned-and-operated stations is an important determinant of which cities experience gasoline price cycles. Since we have identified that cycling began in 2000, one place to look for an explanation of why cycling began in the Midwest would be events that occurred at or around that time that affected market structure. Lewis (2011) links cycling to the presence of QuikTrip and Speedway/SuperAmerica (SSA) in the region. SSA is a subsidiary of Marathon/Ashland petroleum and was formed when Marathon and Ashland merged in 1998.[21] In addition SSA is headquartered in Ohio and our results in Table 2 suggest that cycling may have begun slightly earlier in Ohio than in other parts of the Midwest. The beginning of cycling in the Midwest is also coincident with the price spike and the subsequent short lived unusually low prices in the region in the summer and fall of 2000.[22] It is possible that the combination of the change in market structure along with supply shocks may have lead to this change in pricing dynamic but it would be difficult to show a causal relationship.

Two facts that would have to be incorporated into the explanation of the origins of price cycling are why has cycling persisted for the last decade and why firms, especially the firms with larger market shares, would want to engage in this behavior since average prices declined with the advent of retail price cycling.

---

[21] Taylor and Hosken (2007).
[22] Bulow et al., (2003).

16

References

Allvine, Fred C. and James M. Patterson (1974), *Highway Robbery, An Analysis of the Gasoline Crisis* (Indiana University Press), Chapter 8 & Appendix.

Atkinson, Benjamin (2009), "Retail Gasoline Price Cycles: Evidence from Guelph, Ontario Using Bi-Hourly, Station-Specific Retail Price Data," *Energy Journal* 30: 85-109.

Billingsley, Patrick (1961), *Statistical Inference for Markov Processes* (Chicago University Press).

Bulow, Jeremy, Jeffrey Fischer, Jay Creswell, and Christopher Taylor (2003), "U.S. Midwest Gasoline Pricing and the Spring 2000 Price Spike", *Energy Journal*, 24(3): 121-149.

Castanias, Rick and Herb Johnson (1993), "Gas Wars: Retail Gasoline Price Fluctuations," *Review of Economics and Statistics* 75: 171-74.

Doyle, Joseph, Erich Muehlegger, and Krislert Samphantharak (2010), "Edgeworth Cycles Revisited," *Energy Economics* 32: 651-60.

Eckert, Andrew (2002), "Retail Price Cycles and Response Asymmetry," *Canadian Journal of Economics* 35: 52-77.

Eckert, Andrew (2003), "Retail Price Cycles and the Presence of Small Firms," *International Journal of Industrial Organization* 21: 151-70.

Eckert, Andrew and Douglas S. West (2004), "Retail Gasoline Price Cycles Across Spatially Dispersed Gasoline Stations," *Journal of Law and Economics* 47: 245-73.

Erutku, Can and Vincent A. Hildebrand (2010), "Conspiracy at the Pump," *Journal of Law and Economics* 53: 223-37.

Falk, Barry (1986), "Further Evidence on the Asymmetric Behavior of Economic Time Series Over the Business Cycle," *Journal of Political Economy* 5: 1096-1109.

Lewis, Matthew (2009), "Temporary Wholesale Gasoline Price Spikes have Long-lasting Retail Effects: The Aftermath of Hurricane Rita," *Journal of Law and Economics* 52: 581-605.

Lewis, Matthew (2011), "Price Leadership and Coordination in Retail Gasoline Markets with Price Cycles," working paper.

Lewis, Matthew and Michael Noel (2011), "The Speed of Gasoline Price Response in Markets with and without Edgeworth Cycles," *Review of Economics and Statistics*, forthcoming.

Maskin, Eric and Jean Tirole (1988), "A Theory of Dynamic Oligopoly, II: Price Competition, Kinked Demand Curves, and Edgeworth Cycles," *Econometrica* 56: 571-99.

McQueen, Grant and Steven Thorley (1991), "Are Stock Returns Predictable? A Test Using Markov Chains," *Journal of Finance* 46: 239-63.

Neftçi, Salih N. (1984), "Are Economic Time Series Asymmetric Over the Business Cycle?," *Journal of Political Economy* 2: 307-28.

Noel, Michael D. (2007a), "Edgeworth Price Cycles: Evidence from the Toronto Retail Gasoline Market," *Journal of Industrial Economics* 55: 69-92.

Noel, Michael D. (2007b), "Edgeworth Price Cycles, Cost-Based Pricing, and Sticky Pricing in Retail Gasoline Markets," *Review of Economics and Statistics* 89: 324-34.

Noel, Michael D. (2008), "Edgeworth Cycles and Focal Prices: Computational Dynamic Markov Equilibria," *Journal of Economics and Management Strategy* 17: 345-377.

Noel, Michael D. (2009a), "Do Retail Gasoline Prices Respond Asymmetrically to Cost Shocks? The Influence of Edgeworth Cycles," *RAND Journal of Economics* 40: 582-95.

Noel, Michael D. (2009b), "Edgeworth Cycles and Intertemporal Price Discrimination," working paper.

Rothman, Phillip (2003), "Reconsideration of the Markov Chain Evidence on Unemployment Rate Asymmetry," Department of Economics, East Carolina University, working paper.

Sichel, Daniel E. (1989), "Are Business Cycles Asymmetric? A Correction," *Journal of Political Economy* 5: 1255-1260.

Taylor, Christopher T. and Daniel S. Hosken, (2007), "The Economic Effects of the Marathon Ashland Joint Venture: The Importance of Industry Supply Shocks and Vertical Market Structure," *Journal of Industrial Economics*, 55(3): 419-51.

Wang, Zhongmin (2008), "Collusive Communication and Pricing Coordination in a Retail Gasoline Market," *Review of Industrial Organization* 32: 35-52.

Wang, Zhongmin (2009), "(Mixed) Strategy, Timing and Oligopoly Pricing: Evidence from a Repeated Game in a Timing-Controlled Gasoline Market," *Journal of Political Economy* 117: 987-1030.

Appendix: A Markov-switching model for identifying Edgeworth price cycles

We employ a Markov switching model based upon Neftçi (1984). Let p_t denote the retail price in a given city during week t, which over time is assumed to follow a mean-zero linearly regular stationary process. Define $\{I_t\}$ as a second-order ("two-state") Markov switching process such that

$$
I_t = \begin{cases} +1 & \text{if} & \Delta_t p_t^{(\ell)} > 0 \\ -1 & \text{if} & \Delta_t p_t^{(\ell)} \leq 0, \end{cases}
\tag{4}
$$

where Δ_t denotes the first-difference operator.[23] The associated transition probabilities, denoted λ_{ij} for $i, j = \{0,1\}$, are given by

$$
\left. \begin{aligned}
\lambda_{11} &= \Pr(I_t = +1 \mid I_{t-1} = +1, I_{t-2} = +1) \\[1em]
\lambda_{00} &= \Pr(I_t = -1 \mid I_{t-1} = -1, I_{t-2} = -1) \\[1em]
\lambda_{10} &= \Pr(I_t = +1 \mid I_{t-1} = +1, I_{t-2} = -1) \\[1em]
\lambda_{01} &= \Pr(I_t = -1 \mid I_{t-1} = -1, I_{t-2} = +1)
\end{aligned} \right\}.
\tag{5}
$$

If a city's retail or wholesale gasoline price series exhibits sharp increases and gradual decreases as suggested by the Maskin & Tirole (1988) model of Edgeworth cycles, then $\{I_t\}$ remains in state -1 longer than it remains in state $+1$. In this case, the retail price cycle is said to be *asymmetric* and would imply $\lambda_{00} > \lambda_{11}$. If, on the other hand, the series is *symmetric* over the cycle then $\lambda_{00} = \lambda_{11}$.

Our objective is to obtain estimates of the transition probabilities given in Eq. (5). Let s_T denote a realization of $\{I_t\}$. The log-likelihood function is then given by

$$
\begin{aligned}
L(s_T, \lambda_{11}, \lambda_{00}, \lambda_{10}, \lambda_{01}, \pi_0) = \ & \ln \pi_0 + \phi_{11} \ln \lambda_{11} + \psi_{11} \ln(1 - \lambda_{11}) \\
&+ \phi_{00} \ln \lambda_{00} + \psi_{00} \ln(1 - \lambda_{00}) \\
&+ \phi_{10} \ln \lambda_{10} + \psi_{10} \ln(1 - \lambda_{10}) \\
&+ \phi_{01} \ln \lambda_{01} + \psi_{01} \ln(1 - \lambda_{01}).
\end{aligned}
\tag{6}
$$

The variable π_0 denotes the initial condition (*i.e.*, the probability of observing the initial two states), while the variables $\phi_{11}, \ldots, \psi_{01}$ represent the number of *observed* occurrences of the respective transitions throughout the sample period.

---

[23] As noted by Neftçi (1984, p. 314), an advantage of this procedure is that it can handle nonstationarity in the underlying data (*i.e.*, p_t) given that the implied I_t will often be plausibly stationary even when the former is not.

Neftçi argues that it is necessary to estimate π_0 when the number of observations contained in the relevant time series is small and when the initial state may contain useful information on the transition probabilities (*e.g.*, when the process I_t does not in fact start at $t = 1$, which is usually the case). Neftçi's paper develops a methodology for deriving the limiting probabilities of the initial conditions in terms of the transition probabilities.[24] If, however, the number of observations available in the sample is relatively large (*i.e.*, in an asymptotic sense) the initial state may be treated as a nuisance parameter (Billingsley, 1961). Since the number of daily city-specific price observations available in our dataset covers over a twelve year period (1996-2007), ignoring the influence of the initial condition is likely to be reasonable.[25] With $\pi_0 = 0$, the maximum likelihood estimates (MLEs) of the four unknown parameters $\Lambda = [\lambda_{00}, \lambda_{11}, \lambda_{10}, \lambda_{01}]'$ are obtained by setting the four score equations of the log-likelihood function equal to zero and solving the parameters in terms of the transition counts.[26] The general form of the score equations is given by

$$\frac{\partial L}{\partial \lambda_{ij}} = \frac{\phi_{ij}}{\lambda_{ij}} - \frac{\psi_{ij}}{1 - \lambda_{ij}} = 0. \tag{7}$$

Solving Eq. (7) in terms of λ_{ij} gives

$$\left. \begin{aligned} \frac{\phi_{ij}}{\lambda_{ij}} &= \frac{\psi_{ij}}{1 - \lambda_{ij}} \\ \\ \Rightarrow \phi_{ij}(1 - \lambda_{ij}) &= \psi_{ij}\lambda_{ij} \\ \\ \Rightarrow \lambda_{ij}(\phi_{ij} + \psi_{ij}) &= \phi_{ij} \\ \\ \Rightarrow \lambda_{ij} &= \frac{\phi_{ij}}{\phi_{ij} + \psi_{ij}} = \hat{\lambda}_{ij} \end{aligned} \right\} \tag{8}$$

where $\hat{\lambda}_{ij}$ denotes the (approximate) MLE of λ_{ij}. McQueen and Thorley (1991) show that the asymptotic variance of $\hat{\lambda}_{ij}$ is given by

$$\sigma^2(\hat{\lambda}_{ij}) = \frac{\hat{\lambda}_{ij}(1 - \hat{\lambda}_{ij})}{\phi_{ij} + \psi_{ij}}. \tag{9}$$

---

[24] See Neftçi (1984, pp. 326-327).

[25] Several studies that have relied upon a substantially smaller number of observations than are employed herein have demonstrated that estimating the initial condition along with the transition probabilities does not materially affect the magnitude of the latter when they are estimated alone. *See, e.g.*, Falk (1986) and McQueen and Thorley (1991). Further, a particular advantage of treating π_0 as a nuisance parameter comes from the considerable reduction in the computation burden of estimating the transition probabilities (Rothman, 2003). Specifically, ignoring the initial state variables does not require using nonlinear numerical methods to approximate the maximum of the log-likelihood function. Rather, as demonstrated below, closed-form analytical solutions for the maximum likelihood estimators are easily obtained.

[26] McQueen and Thorley (1991, p. 243).

Testing for the presence of Edgeworth price cycles (asymmetry) in gasoline prices involves testing the null hypothesis $H_0 : \lambda_{00} = \lambda_{11}$ against the (two-sided) alternative $H_1 : \lambda_{00} \neq \lambda_{11}$.

Hypothesis Testing

Neftçi demonstrates how the test for asymmetry can be evaluated by using the estimate of the transition probabilities to construct a confidence region (ellipsoid), the center of which corresponds to the MLEs of λ_{11} and λ_{00}. All points within the confidence ellipsoid represent the true value of the latter estimate for a given confidence level.[27] However, Sichel (1989) demonstrates that this procedure "has low power and is sensitive to noise" (p. 1259). Specifically, he shows that Neftçi's test may fail to identify asymmetry that is actually present, and instead applies an asymptotic *t*-test that appears to give higher power.

McQueen and Thorley (1991) test the symmetry hypothesis in their data by considering asymptotic Lagrange Multiplier, Likelihood Ratio, and Wald tests (all of which are approximately equal for large sample sizes). They note that: "The choice of test statistics is normally a matter of computational convenience" (p. 256). Again, the length of our time series data suggests that we can rely upon the direct analytical solutions for the MLEs and (asymptotic) variances of the Markov transition probabilities. This fact motivates the use of the Wald test since it uses the MLEs and asymptotic variance estimates of the *unconstrained* log-likelihood function, which correspond to the "unrestricted" estimates obtained by appealing to Eqs. (8) and (9). The computed value the Wald test under H_0 is given by:

$$\frac{(\hat{\lambda}_{00} - \hat{\lambda}_{11})^2}{\sigma(\hat{\lambda}_{11}) - \sigma(\hat{\lambda}_{00})} \sim \chi^2_{df=1}. \tag{10}$$

This test statistics is used to determine whether there is a statistically significant Edgeworth price cycling effect within a given city over the sample period.

---

[27] *See* Neftçi (1984, pp. 315-318) for the formula used to construct the confidence ellipsoid and further discussion of this test.

Figure 1
Ohio Metro Areas Monthly Median First Difference of Retail Price
1998 - 2003

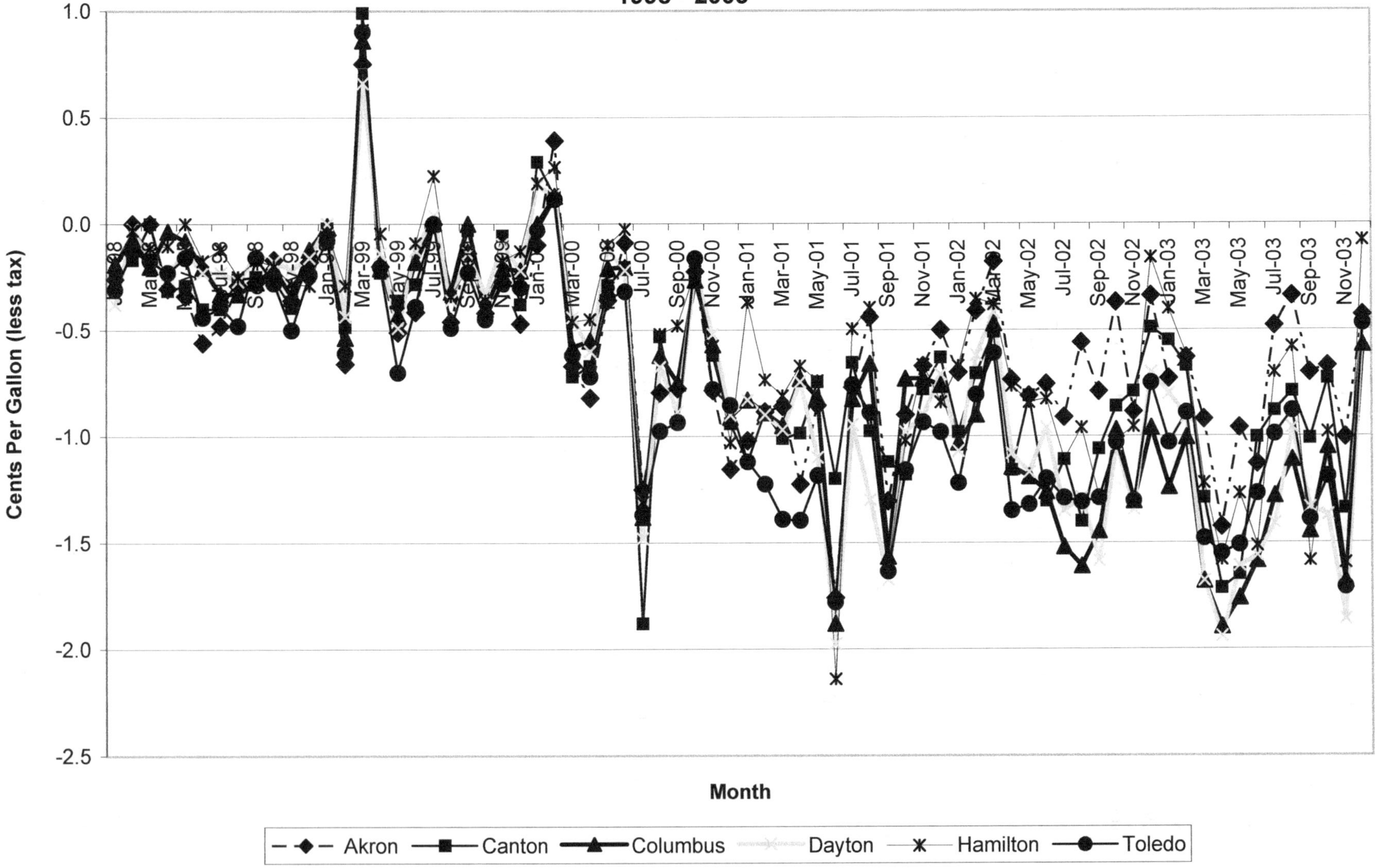
1.0
0.5
0.0
-0.5
-1.0
-1.5
-2.0
-2.5
Cents Per Gallon (less tax)
Mar-99
May-99
Mar-00
Jul-00
Sep-00
Nov-00
Jan-01
Mar-01
May-01
Jul-01
Sep-01
Nov-01
Jan-02
May-02
Jul-02
Sep-02
Nov-02
Jan-03
Mar-03
May-03
Jul-03
Sep-03
Nov-03
Month
Akron
Canton
Columbus
Dayton
Hamilton
Toledo

Table 1. Descriptive statistics - state locations and prices

Padd	State	No. of Cities	1996-2007 Mean Price	1996-2007 Median 1st Diff	1996-99 Mean Price	1996-99 Median 1st Diff	2001-2007 Mean Price	2001-2007 Median 1st Diff
ALL		350	124.84	-0.05	75.54	-0.01	154.48	-0.10
Padd 1a		18	127.22	0.00	77.44	0.00	156.85	-0.01
(New England)	CT	4	127.02	0.00	76.36	0.00	157.01	-0.02
	MA	4	130.32	-0.01	80.45	0.00	159.91	-0.03
	ME	4	125.69	0.00	77.63	0.00	154.52	0.02
	NH	4	125.21	0.00	74.97	0.00	155.08	0.00
	RI	1	125.10	-0.01	76.01	-0.01	154.25	-0.03
	VT	1	131.91	0.00	80.27	0.00	162.99	0.00
Padd 1b		44	123.81	0.00	74.28	0.00	153.56	-0.01
(Central Atlantic)	DC	1	136.88	0.01	80.82	0.00	171.39	0.04
	DE	2	123.40	0.00	73.51	0.00	153.25	0.01
	MD	5	125.02	0.00	74.25	0.00	155.56	-0.01
	NJ	9	127.14	0.00	76.91	0.00	157.08	-0.01
	NY	13	125.36	0.00	75.85	0.00	155.22	-0.01
	PA	14	118.93	-0.01	70.78	0.00	147.86	-0.03
Padd 1c		58	120.52	-0.02	70.98	0.00	150.39	-0.05
(Lower Atlantic)	FL	19	120.93	-0.01	71.19	0.00	151.09	-0.03
	GA	7	119.01	-0.03	70.14	0.00	148.49	-0.08
	NC	11	118.93	-0.01	69.67	0.00	148.48	-0.04
	SC	8	119.90	-0.01	70.26	0.00	149.80	-0.05
	VA	8	121.65	-0.01	72.44	0.00	151.21	-0.02
	WV	5	123.74	-0.07	73.10	0.00	154.19	-0.16
Padd 2		108	122.55	-0.13	73.20	-0.04	152.20	-0.31
(Midwest)	IA	8	123.53	-0.04	72.76	-0.01	154.27	-0.08
	IL	10	121.26	-0.15	73.40	-0.04	149.87	-0.38
	IN	13	120.92	-0.25	72.32	-0.06	149.94	-0.66
	KS	4	119.82	-0.13	70.93	-0.04	149.33	-0.23
	KY	7	125.02	-0.20	75.56	-0.03	154.96	-0.49
	MI	9	122.13	-0.34	71.78	-0.11	152.15	-0.75
	MN	4	127.05	-0.15	79.01	-0.04	156.17	-0.38
	MO	6	119.96	-0.13	70.31	-0.06	149.76	-0.25
	ND	3	128.88	0.00	80.33	0.00	158.35	0.00
	NE	2	123.78	-0.05	72.49	-0.02	154.60	-0.10
	OH	15	122.43	-0.34	73.40	-0.09	151.76	-0.79
	OK	5	120.36	-0.04	70.71	-0.02	150.49	-0.09
	SD	2	128.37	0.00	78.99	0.00	158.07	-0.02
	TN	7	120.20	-0.02	71.52	0.00	149.62	-0.06
	WI	13	123.89	-0.02	73.37	-0.02	154.23	-0.04
Padd 3		59	121.27	-0.03	72.57	0.00	150.70	-0.06
(Gulf Coast)	AL	11	121.68	-0.02	72.85	0.00	151.18	-0.06
	AR	6	119.12	-0.02	69.96	0.00	148.76	-0.07
	LA	8	122.63	-0.01	74.29	0.00	151.80	-0.02
	MS	4	121.43	-0.01	73.50	0.00	150.26	-0.05
	NM	3	131.49	-0.04	81.38	-0.01	162.15	-0.08
	TX	27	120.02	-0.04	71.42	-0.01	149.41	-0.08
Padd 4		16	128.00	-0.02	81.08	-0.01	156.29	-0.03
(Rocky Mountain)	CO	7	128.30	-0.05	79.93	-0.04	157.56	-0.07
	ID	2	129.93	0.00	82.85	0.00	157.50	0.01
	MT	3	127.48	0.00	83.62	0.00	154.11	0.02
	UT	2	125.88	-0.03	79.63	-0.02	153.93	-0.03
	WY	2	127.89	0.00	81.11	-0.01	156.19	0.00

Padd	State	No. of Cities	1996-2007		1996-99		2001-2007	
			Mean Price	Median 1st Diff	Mean Price	Median 1st Diff	Mean Price	Median 1st Diff
Padd 5		47	138.87	-0.03	88.83	-0.03	168.85	-0.03
(West Coast)	AK	1	148.29	-0.01	98.22	0.00	178.86	-0.05
	AZ	5	137.37	-0.03	88.65	-0.02	166.97	-0.03
	CA	25	141.13	-0.04	89.55	-0.04	171.91	-0.05
	HI	1	148.37	0.00	102.11	-0.01	177.47	0.03
	NV	2	134.29	-0.02	83.97	0.00	164.32	-0.02
	OR	4	136.98	-0.03	89.64	-0.03	165.29	-0.03
	WA	9	133.18	-0.01	85.16	-0.01	161.92	-0.01

Table 2. Cities with one or more years of cycling based on the median first difference in price

	Median First Difference in Price									2001-07	
	1996-99	2000	2001	2002	2003	2004	2005	2006	2007	Median ≤ -.05	Markov Test
ILLINOIS											
Bloomington-Normal	0.01	-0.24	-0.66	-0.48	-0.63	-0.50	-0.73	-0.70	-0.64	yes	**
Champaign-Urbana	-0.01	-0.11	-0.44	-0.47	-0.49	-0.33	-0.57	-0.52	-0.50		**
Chicago	0.01	-0.08	-0.50	-0.24	-0.34	-0.26	-0.27	-0.22	-0.26		*
Decatur	-0.03	-0.39	-0.39	-0.40	-0.43	-0.30	-0.46	-0.57	-0.52		**
Peoria-Pekin	-0.04	-0.25	-0.77	-0.62	-0.59	-0.22	-0.40	-0.43	-0.30		**
Rockford	0.00	-0.13	-0.74	-0.72	-0.45	-0.35	-0.73	-0.43	-0.49	yes	**
Springfield	-0.04	-0.28	-1.13	-0.69	-0.90	-0.63	-0.74	-0.93	-1.21	yes	**
INDIANA											
Bloomington	0.00	-0.13	-0.26	-0.44	-0.47	-0.66	-0.60	-0.69	-0.87	yes	**
Cincinnati	0.00	0.01	-0.11	-0.09	-0.34	-0.40	-0.57	-0.41	-0.33		*
Elkhart-Goshen	-0.01	-0.26	-0.59	-0.68	-0.73	-0.73	-0.89	-1.13	-0.98	yes	**
Evansville-Henderson	0.00	-0.32	-0.42	-0.21	-0.11	-0.20	-0.31	-0.46	-0.76		*
Fort Wayne	-0.01	-0.49	-0.84	-0.83	-0.65	-0.66	-0.80	-0.83	-0.92	yes	**
Gary	0.00	-0.29	-0.70	-0.54	-0.67	-0.64	-0.75	-0.67	-0.75	yes	**
Indianapolis	0.00	-0.24	-0.85	-0.95	-1.20	-1.29	-1.23	-1.31	-1.38	yes	**
Kokomo	0.03	-0.19	-0.56	-0.38	-0.47	-0.54	-0.60	-0.66	-0.87	yes	**
Lafayette	0.01	-0.19	-0.50	-0.61	-0.66	-0.60	-0.72	-0.79	-0.79	yes	**
Louisville	0.03	-0.24	-0.49	-0.37	-0.59	-0.33	-0.45	-0.54	-0.55	yes	**
Muncie	-0.06	-0.32	-0.54	-0.53	-0.76	-0.93	-0.67	-1.10	-1.19	yes	**
South Bend	-0.01	-0.29	-0.69	-0.63	-0.59	-0.60	-0.88	-1.01	-0.97	yes	**
Terre Haute	-0.07	-0.30	-0.43	-0.43	-0.51	-0.31	-0.31	-0.55	-0.58		**
KANSAS											
Wichita	-0.17	-0.19	-0.51	-0.26	-0.30	-0.45	-0.52	-0.61	-0.59		**
KENTUCKY											
Cincinnati	0.03	-0.18	-0.45	-0.50	-0.92	-0.68	-0.81	-0.75	-0.57	yes	**
Evansville-Henderson	0.00	-0.13	-0.18	-0.10	-0.08	-0.06	-0.27	-0.54	-0.89		**
Huntington-Ashland	0.00	-0.32	-0.63	-0.20	-0.41	-0.41	-0.62	-0.61	-0.60		**
Lexington	0.01	-0.23	-0.62	-0.47	-0.81	-1.04	-1.00	-1.46	-1.43	yes	**
Louisville	0.06	-0.29	-0.61	-0.41	-0.87	-0.59	-0.85	-1.45	-1.71	yes	**
MICHIGAN											
Ann Arbor	0.01	-0.16	-0.50	-0.36	-0.51	-0.44	-0.50	-0.60	-0.35	yes	**
Benton Harbor	-0.04	-0.12	-0.55	-0.33	-0.52	-0.48	-0.54	-0.75	-0.73	yes	**
Flint	-0.11	-0.42	-1.00	-0.83	-1.03	-1.01	-1.10	-1.26	-1.25	yes	**
Grand Rapids-Muskegon-Holland	-0.11	-0.39	-0.79	-0.57	-0.84	-1.02	-1.30	-1.41	-1.46	yes	**
Jackson	-0.10	-0.35	-0.69	-0.66	-0.72	-0.71	-0.91	-0.99	-0.79	yes	**
Kalamazoo-Battle Creek	-0.03	-0.34	-0.85	-0.55	-0.72	-0.76	-0.90	-1.06	-1.07	yes	**
Lansing-East Lansing	-0.02	-0.41	-1.07	-0.79	-0.95	-1.17	-1.31	-1.52	-1.42	yes	**
Saginaw-Bay City-Midland	-0.10	-0.42	-1.01	-0.75	-0.76	-1.05	-1.22	-1.28	-1.42	yes	**

Median First Difference in Price

	1996-99	2000	2001	2002	2003	2004	2005	2006	2007	2001-07 Median ≤ -.05	Markov Test
MINNESOTA											
Minneapolis-St. Paul	-0.03	-0.23	-0.81	-0.77	-1.14	-0.97	-0.98	-1.05	-0.99	yes	**
Rochester	0.00	-0.01	-0.58	-0.37	-0.42	-0.42	-0.29	-0.24	-0.09		**
St. Cloud	0.01	-0.21	-0.69	-0.14	-0.19	-0.12	-0.15	-0.44	-0.45		
MISSOURI											
Kansas City	-0.05	-0.21	-0.50	-0.21	-0.29	-0.33	-0.32	-0.38	-0.20		*
St. Louis	-0.07	-0.22	-0.58	-0.50	-0.67	-0.81	-0.94	-0.62	-0.62	yes	**
OHIO											
Akron	-0.01	-0.64	-0.88	-0.57	-0.78	-0.85	-0.87	-1.11	-1.06	yes	**
Canton-Massillon	-0.05	-0.59	-1.01	-0.98	-1.01	-0.98	-1.18	-1.22	-1.35	yes	**
Cincinnati	0.00	-0.41	-0.91	-0.95	-1.24	-1.15	-1.46	-1.43	-1.51	yes	**
Cleveland-Lorain-Elyria	0.00	-0.38	-0.77	-0.80	-0.94	-1.04	-1.17	-0.99	-0.98	yes	**
Columbus	-0.01	-0.50	-0.84	-1.11	-1.32	-1.47	-1.57	-1.47	-1.43	yes	**
Dayton-Springfield	0.00	-0.53	-1.01	-1.07	-1.37	-1.33	-1.51	-1.68	-1.60	yes	**
Hamilton-Middletown	0.00	-0.42	-0.81	-0.75	-1.12	-1.16	-1.42	-1.60	-1.73	yes	**
Lima	0.00	-0.39	-0.71	-0.54	-0.90	-0.94	-0.85	-1.11	-1.00	yes	**
Mansfield	0.05	-0.43	-0.93	-0.75	-0.78	-1.06	-0.76	-0.92	-0.78	yes	**
Parkersburg-Marietta	0.04	-0.23	-0.36	-0.15	-0.25	-0.19	-0.19	-0.60	-0.20		*
Steubenville-Weirton	0.01	-0.16	-0.26	-0.08	-0.17	-0.30	-0.63	-0.59	-0.40		**
Toledo	-0.03	-0.61	-1.17	-1.13	-1.15	-1.59	-1.42	-1.51	-1.30	yes	**
WEST VIRGINIA											
Huntington-Ashland	0.00	-0.13	-0.31	0.03	-0.24	-0.28	-0.34	-0.59	-0.60		**

Table 3. Effect of cycling on price levels

Dependent variable = Price of Regular	(1)	(2)	(3)	(4)	(5)	(6)	(7)	(8)
Cycle * After	-1.14*	-0.74	-1.05*	-0.68	-1.42*	-1.32*	-0.94*	-0.74
	(1.67)	(1.13)	(1.76)	(1.18)	(1.87)	(1.93)	(1.70)	(1.33)
Cycle	-0.46	-0.43	-0.39	0.39	-0.67	-0.40	0.13	0.27
	(0.34)	(0.34)	(0.33)	(0.32)	(0.45)	(0.28)	(0.10)	(0.20)
After	9.58***	9.53***	9.60***	9.54***	11.11***	11.071***	10.48***	-8.77***
	(17.58)	(17.48)	(17.35)	(17.20)	(21.40)	(22.56)	(10.48)	(16.27)
Constant	116.24***	106.39***	116.23***	106.38***	86.48***	82.21***	86.72***	106.55***
	(200.12)	(191.98)	(198.47)	(190.64)	(224.81)	(267.18)	(288.64)	(334.08)
Data Set	1996-2010	1996-2007	1996-2010	1996-2007	1996-2010	1996-2007	1996-2010	1996-2007
State / Year Fixed Effects	Yes	Yes	Yes	Yes	Yes	Yes	Yes	Yes
Definiton of Cycle City	Markov 5%	Markov 5%	Markov 10%	Markov 10%	Markov 5%	Markov 5%	Markov 10%	Markov 10%
Observations	1,828,374	1,444,851	1,828,374	1,444,851	563,947	445,637	872,348	689,376
Number of States/District (for Clusters)	51	51	51	51	15	15	21	21
Number of cities	350	350	350	350	108	108	167	167
R-squared	0.86	0.9	0.86	0.9	0.86	0.89	0.86	0.86

Notes: All estimates reflect MSA-level data. Absolute t-statistics reflecting clustered standard errors at the state level are shown in parentheses.

"*" = statistical significance at the 10 percent level in a two-tailed test

"**" = statistical significance at the 5 percent level in a two-tailed test

"***" = statistical significance at the 1 percent level in a two-tailed test

Table 4. Effect of station ownership characteristics on the presence of retail price cycling (Probit regressions)

Dependent variable = Cycle indicator [based on Markov model]	(1)	(2)	(3)	(4)
HHI - refiner company owned & operated sites	1.250** (2.50)		1.424** (2.01)	1.516** (2.08)
Market share - refiner company owned & operated sites		0.036 (0.08)	0.067 (0.13)	0.670 (0.86)
HHI - independent and jobber sites	1.440 (0.41)		3.13438 (0.87)	4.250 (1.09)
Market share - independent and jobber sites		1.270** (2.19)	1.366** (2.11)	2.075** (2.25)
Median household income				-2.96E-05 (1.50)
Population density				1.290E-05 (0.04)
Total population				4.647E-04 (0.51)
Prob > Wald Chi-squared (Null: Coefficients are jointly zero)	0.0434	0.0481	0.0912	0.0991
Pseudo R-squared	0.1231	0.1416	0.2582	0.3057

Notes: All estimates reflect MSA-level data. Absolute t-statistics reflecting robust (heteroskedasticity-consistent) standard errors are shown in parentheses. The number of observations in each column is 31.

"*" = statistical significance at the 10 percent level in a two-tailed test

"**" = statistical significance at the 5 percent level in a two-tailed test

"***" = statistical significance at the 1 percent level in a two-tailed test